# Keys to Listening Success

場面・機能・音変化で学ぶ実践リスニング

by

**Koji Nishiya**
**Tom Dillon**

JN034086

TSURUMI SHOTEN

**Keys to Listening Success**

写真クレジット一覧:
© HosonoAtsuo: p. 2, p. 4(下), p. 7, p. 14(下), p. 21, p. 22,
p. 29(上), p. 36, p. 44(上), p. 46, p. 60(下), p. 64(上)

## 自習用音声について

本書の自習用音声は以下よりダウンロードできます。予習、復習に
ご利用ください。
(2022 年 4 月 1 日開始予定)

http://www.otowatsurumi.com/0547

URL はブラウザのアドレスバーに直接入力して下さい。
パソコンでのご利用をお勧めします。圧縮ファイル (zip) ですのでスマート
フォンでの場合は事前に解凍アプリをご用意下さい。

# まえがき

## 学生の皆さんへ

　2020 年から 2021 年の 2 年間（執筆時現在、まだ現在進行形）、世界中で猛威を振るった新型コロナ肺炎は、社会と人びとの暮らしに大きな影響をもたらしました。学生生活についても、大学の授業がオンラインになったり、通常授業と併せて行うハイブリッド授業になったり、それに伴って、先生や友だちとの直接コミュニケーションが大きく減ったのではないでしょうか。

　そのような中、私たちは皆、コミュニケーションの大切さについて、折に触れて、いろいろな点から考える機会に恵まれました。ヒトが誕生するとき、胎児が初めて聞くのは、母親の心臓の鼓動や血液の流れる音と言われています。そこまで遡らなくても、ことばによるコミュニケーションにおいても、「音」がはじめです。文字がない音はあっても、音を伴わない文字はないのです。

　私が 20 代に英語教材の編集者をしていたころ、元アメリカ応用言語学会会長の高名な先生のレクチャーを直接お聞きする機会に恵まれたことがあります。プアな英語力しか持ち合わせていなかったので、どこまで理解できたのか心もとないのですが、いまでも記憶として残っているのは、Listening is the foundation of learning English. ということばです。別にそんなエピソードを持ち出さなくとも、当たり前のこと、とお叱りを受けるかもしれませんが、いずれにしても、本教材の作成にあたり、リスニングにおける「音」の重要性をどのように自然な形で盛り込むか、考えました。

　各ユニットに「シチュエーション、トピック的な項目」と「機能的な項目」という 2 種類の要素を配しましたが、さらに、英語のリスニングで日本人が不得意と言われている「音の変化」を学習する要素を加えました。ことばで説明するよりも、教材の中で学習したほうが理解しやすいので詳しくは述べませんが、簡単に言うと、2 つの音が干渉して音に変化が起きる、というもので、これは何度も音を聴いて、まねて何度も発話して身に付けるほかありません。正しく発話できるようになれば、英語を正しく聴き取れるようになります。ですから、リスニングの教材ですが、「何度も聴いて、何度も発話する」、ここまでやって効果がでることを忘れないでください。

　本教材で扱ったキーフレーズは、トピック的な項目や、機能的な項目に関するごくごく一部です。本教材をきっかけに、上に説明したやり方で、興味ある分野のいろいろな英語素材へ対象を広げていくことで、皆さんのリスニング力が伸びていけばうれしい限りです。

　2021 年　秋

編著者代表　西 谷 恒 志

# 教材の構成と利用法

## ● 全 Unit の構成

全体で 15 の Unit から成り、各 Unit は 2 つの Section で構成されています。Section A は「シチュエーション・トピック」シラバス、Section B は「ノーション・ファンクション」シラバスを採用しています。

| Unit | §A（Situation / Topic） | §B（Notion / Function） |
|------|------------------------|-------------------------|
| 1 | 健康 | 場所・方向など |
| 2 | 家庭・家事 | 時（の長さ）・頻度 |
| 3 | 電話 | 数量 |
| 4 | 学校 | 感情 |
| 5 | 交通・運輸 | 賛成・反対；同意・不同意 |
| 6 | 天候・自然 | 評価・比較など |
| 7 | ショッピング | 計画・予定 |
| 8 | スポーツ | 情報のやりとり |
| 9 | レストラン・食事 | 方法・手段 |
| 10 | 空港・フライト | 原因・結果；目的・理由；場合 |
| 11 | インターネット・IT | 依頼・命令・要求 |
| 12 | ソーシャルライフ・SNS | 義務・必要 |
| 13 | 芸術・エンターテインメント | 可能・困難など |
| 14 | 旅行・ホテル | 変化・移動・統一など |
| 15 | ビジネス・オフィス | 金銭関係 |

## ● 各 Unit の構成と学習法　　＊🎧は自習用音声収録箇所

Section A/B ともに

### Key Words and Expressions: 🎧

① テキストを見ながら音声を聴く。

② テキストを見ながら、音声にかぶせるように声を出して音読する（覚えられるまで何度も行う）。

③ テキストを見ないで、音声にかぶせるように声を出して音読する（できないときは②に戻る）。

### Training 1: 🎧

Key Words and Expressions の語句・表現を含んだ 2 行会話です。音声として耳で正しく捉えられるか、空所に語句・表現を書き入れて行うトレーニングです。一度で聴き取れなければ、2，3 回聴いても構いません。

## Training 2: 🎧

Key Words and Expressions の語句・表現を、Training 1 よりも長い会話、あるいは、パッセージで聴き、全体の意味を捉えるトレーニングです。正しく聴き取れたかどうか、Question に答えて確認します。

## Practice for Sound Change: 🎧

英語の音変化を「連結（リンキング）」「脱落（リダクション）」「同化」「フラッピング」の4つに分けて、例文とともにトレーニングします。

① テキストを見ながら音声を聴く。

② テキストを見ながら、音声にかぶせるように声を出して音読する（覚えられるまで何度も行う）。

③ テキストを見ないで、音声にかぶせるように声を出して音読する（できないときは②に戻る）。

## Exercises: （Exercises の音声は教授用 CD にだけ収録されています。）

Unit の総仕上げです。

1. はディクテーション。Practice for Sound Change で取り上げた音変化を含む英文を聴いて、空所に語句を書き入れます。

2. は TOEIC の Part 1（写真描写問題）形式の問題、2問。Section A に関連した問題と Section B に関連した問題があります。

3. は TOEIC の Part 2（応答問題）形式の問題、3問。Section A に関連した問題と Section B に関連した問題が含まれています。

4. は TOEIC の Part 3（会話問題）形式のミニ問題。会話文も短く、質問文も2問だけです。Section A、あるいは、Section B に関連しています。

5. は TOEIC の Part 4（説明文問題）形式のミニ問題。問題文も短く、質問文も2問だけです。Section A、あるいは、Section B に関連しています。

なお、Exercise 4 と Exercise 5 は巻末の解答用紙を利用して解答提出用問題とすることができます。

## ★ 音声の記号とトラック番号について

 1 ～ 🎧 105　自習用音声のトラック番号です。

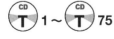 1 ～ 🅣 75　　教授用 CD（各ユニットの Exercises の音声を収録）のトラック番号です。

※録音された音声は、アメリカ人男性とイギリス人女性によるものです。

# CONTENTS

# UNIT 1

# Why don't you get some rest?

## Points

このユニットでは、「健康」に関する語句・表現と、「場所・方向など」に関する語句・表現を聴き取る練習を行います。

## Section A Health [健康]

### ❏ Key Words and Expressions

1

1. Injure / be injured; Recovery / Recover （〜を痛める／けがをする；回復／回復する）
   A: I hear you <u>injured</u> your knee. Can you play in the tournament?
   B: No, the doctor says full <u>recovery</u> takes two months.

2. Feel tired [dizzy / sick / depressed, etc.] （だるい［目まいがする／体調が悪い／気が重い］など）
   A: I <u>feel</u> a little <u>sick</u>.
   B: Why don't you get some rest?

3. On medication / Take medicine （薬を飲んでいる／薬を飲む）
   I have high cholesterol but I'm not <u>on medication</u>. I just watch what I eat.

4. See a doctor （医者に診てもらう）
   There is no quick cure for depression. Victims should <u>see a doctor</u> and try to take things easy.

5. Suffer from （〜を患う）
   I <u>suffer from</u> hay fever but have never been treated for it.

6. Take it easy （休む、くつろぐ）
   If you don't feel well, try to <u>take it easy</u>. Don't overdo it.

1

## ❑ *Training A-1*:

2

音声を聴いて空所に正しい語句を書き入れなさい。

1. A: Lately, I've been (                ) fatigue.
   B: You should (            ). I think you are working too hard.

2. A: After exercising, I (            ).
   B: Hmm. Maybe you should (         ).

3. A: I (           ) last winter and it hurts even now.
   B: (      ) can take time. Are you (           ) for the pain?

## ❑ *Training A-2*:

3

会話文を聴き、その会話に関する質問文の答えとして最も適切なものを (A)〜(D) より選びなさい。

Question: What is the man most worried about?
   (A) Whether he can get an appointment
   (B) His heart condition
   (C) If he can find a seat
   (D) If a nurse will examine him

## Section B **Location/Directions** [場所・方向]

## ❑ *Key Words and Expressions*

4

1. **Can't miss** （見逃すことがない、すぐに見つかる）
   You <u>can't miss</u> the hotel. It's halfway between the park and the train station.

2. **~ Minutes away** （〜分離れて）
   The nearest hospital is over thirty <u>minutes away</u>.

3. **On / Near / Close to / Next to / Between** （〜の上に／〜の近くに／
   〜のすぐ隣に／〜の間に）
   The men's room is located <u>on</u> the first floor, <u>next to</u> the rear exit.

4. **Front / Rear** （前面、正面／後部、背面）
   The restrooms are in the <u>rear</u> of the store.

2

5. **Rural / Urban** (いなかの／都会の)

We live in a quiet <u>rural</u> community.

6. **Turn right [left] / Take a right [left] turn** (右 [左] に曲がる／右 [左] 折する)

<u>Turn left</u> at the stoplight. You'll see the stadium in the distance.

## ❏ *Training B-1*:

5

音声を聴いて空所に正しい語句を書き入れなさい。

1. A: Could you tell me how to get to the public library?

   B: (                ) at the second corner and you (            ).

2. A: Where is Mr. Johnson's office?

   B: (       ) the fourth floor (       ) the lounge.

3. A: What's been the key to your shop's success?

   B: Location! We're only (              ) the subway line.

## ❏ *Training B-2*:

6

会話文を聴き、その会話に関する質問文の答えとして最も適切なものを (A)〜(D) より選びなさい。

Question: **Why did the speaker drive two hours to a hotel?**

    (A) There was no hotel in Middleville.

    (B) He had to wait for his car to be repaired.

    (C) He was tired of staying in the park.

    (D) He needed to locate a repair shop.

## **Practice for Sound Change:** [音変化に慣れよう]

「破裂音 [p, b; t, d; k, g] ＋母音」の音変化の第 1 回目です。

1. Don't be afraid of speaking in <u>front of</u> people.
2. Many workers are <u>concerned about</u> their mental health.
3. The first <u>job of an</u> academic counselor is to <u>look up</u> each student's <u>record of</u> achievement.
4. The muscles that <u>make up</u> your <u>back and</u> shoulders should be <u>stretched every</u> day.
5. Technological advances in the medical field may one day <u>sweep away</u> cancer <u>and other</u> illnesses.

# Exercises

**1.** 次の (1)〜(5) の英文を聴き取り、それぞれの空所に語句を書き入れなさい。

(1) (                         ) I'll be right there.

(2) He plays the piano and enjoys (                       ).

(3) It's easy to (                      ) by either bus or automobile.

(4) Covid-19 recovery will (               ), according to the public health center.

(5) Patients will be (               ), depending on the (     ) disorder they have.

**2.** 次の (1), (2) の写真について、それぞれの写真を説明する英文が 4 つ聞こえてきます。最も適切な英文の記号を◯で囲みなさい。

(1)

(A)　　(B)　　(C)　　(D)

(2)

(A)　　(B)　　(C)　　(D)

**3.** 1.〜3. の英文につづいて、(A), (B), (C) の 3 つの応答文が聞こえます。それぞれの英文の
応答文として最も適切な応答文の記号を○で囲みなさい。

1. (A)　(B)　(C)
2. (A)　(B)　(C)
3. (A)　(B)　(C)

（Exercise 4 と Exercise 5 は解答提出用問題です）

**4.** 会話文を聴き、その会話に関する質問文 (1), (2) の答えとして最も適切なものを (A)〜(D)
より選び、巻末解答用紙の記号を○で囲みなさい。

(1) **What does the man need?**
   (A) He needs an eye doctor.
   (B) He needs help at work.
   (C) He needs more medication.
   (D) He needs to run faster.

(2) **Why can't the man visit his doctor?**
   (A) He doesn't have enough medication.
   (B) The doctor is at work.
   (C) He doesn't have enough time.
   (D) His doctor is too busy.

**5.** 英文を聴き、その英文に関する質問文 (3), (4) の答えとして最も適切なものを (A)〜(D) よ
り選び、巻末解答用紙の記号を○で囲みなさい。

(3) **What is the speaker explaining?**
   (A) How to get around the building
   (B) How a new employee should begin his/her work
   (C) How the manager runs the business
   (D) How to get to the customer's service desk

(4) **Where do employees put on their uniforms?**
   (A) At the customer's service desk
   (B) In the changing room
   (C) In their locker
   (D) At the rear entrance

# Unit 2

# Today is a nice day to hang out the laundry.

## Points

このユニットでは、「家庭・家事」に関する語句・表現と、「時（の長さ）・頻度」に関する
語句・表現を聴き取る練習を行います。

## Section A Family; Household Chores [家庭・家事]

### ❏ *Key Words and Expressions*

8

1. **Clean the house / Clean *one's* room**（家の掃除をする／〜の部屋を掃除する）
   Mom says Dad hasn't <u>cleaned his room</u> for a year.

2. **Clear [Set] the table**（テーブルの皿を片付ける［皿を（テーブルに）並べる］）
   Can you <u>set the table</u> for supper?

3. **Do the laundry [wash / ironing]**（洗たくをする／アイロンをかける）
   I have almost nothing to wear! I haven't <u>done the laundry</u> for ten days!

4. **Hang out the laundry**（洗たく物を干す）
   Today is a nice day to <u>hang out the laundry</u>.

5. **Make dinner [supper]**（夕食を作る）
   I'd rather <u>make dinner</u> than buy it at a convenience store.

6. **Wash the dishes [windows]**（皿洗いをする／窓を洗う）
   My wife usually <u>washes the dishes</u> and I dry.

## ❏ *Training A-1* :

9

音声を聴いて空所に正しい語句を書き入れなさい。

**1.** A: Can you (               ) tonight? I feel a little tired.
     B: Sure. You take it easy and I'll (         ).

**2.** A: Jimmy! You need to (         )!
     B: I did it while you were (         ).

**3.** A: I don't mind (         ), but I dislike (     ).
     B: Me too. I would rather wear wrinkled clothes.

## ❏ *Training A-2* :

10

会話文を聴き、その会話に関する質問文の答えとして最も適切なものを (A) 〜 (D) より選びなさい。

Question: Where does the mother think her son will find his missing sock?
    (A) In his room
    (B) In the laundry
    (C) With her clothes
    (D) Outside

## Section B　Time/Length of Time/Frequency

［時（の長さ）・頻度］

## ❏ *Key Words and Expressions*

11

**1. At the end of**（〜の終わりに）
The paper is due <u>at the end of</u> the term.

**2. At the moment**（今のところ、ちょうど今）
We are all sold out <u>at the moment</u>.

**3. During**（〜の間ずっと、〜の間に）
There was a power outage <u>during</u> the game.

**4. On occasion**（時々、状況によって）
Typically, I take the train, but I will drive to work <u>on occasion</u>.

**5. Recently**（最近）

Recently I've had trouble sleeping.

**6. While ...**（～の間に）

Your boss telephoned while you were away.

## ❏ *Training* **B-1**:

12

音声を聴いて空所に正しい語句を書き入れなさい。

**1.** A: The doctor is too busy to see you (            ).
   B: That's okay. I'll read a magazine (        ).

**2.** A: Have you seen any good movies (     )?
   B: No, I only go to the theater (      ).

**3.** A: Business is usually good (       ).
   B: Especially this year. I'm looking forward to the sales report (         ).

## ❏ *Training* **B-2**:

13

英文を聴き、その英文に関する質問文の答えとして最も適切なものを (A)～(D) より選びなさい。

**Question: Why are sales totals unclear at the moment?**
   (A) The branch managers haven't had time to check.
   (B) Totals only come at the end of the month.
   (C) Impressions are usually correct.
   (D) Sales have been strong recently.

14

┌─ *Practice for* **S**ound **C**hange: ［音変化に慣れよう］ 連 結 ② ─┐

「破裂音 [p, b; t, d; k, g] ＋母音」の音変化の第 2 回目です。

**1.** Please keep in touch while you are studying abroad.
**2.** The neighboring houses put on an incredible display of Christmas lights.
**3.** The recipe calls for the meat to be boiled in soy sauce for five minutes.
**4.** The flight to Bangkok took off at the scheduled time.
**5.** My six-year-old son gave me a drawing of the cake he wanted.

# Exercises

**1.** 次の (1)〜(5) の英文を聴き取り、それぞれの空所に語句を書き入れなさい。

(1)  His mother told him to (　　　　　　　　　　) before dinner.

(2)  Her entire family called her "Si-Si" (　　　　　　　) her given name.

(3)  Please let me know the average (　　　　　　　) for a family of four.

(4)  Sometimes body image problems may (　　　　　　　　　　) who maintain a healthy weight.

(5)  The primary information to obtain when (　　　　　　　　　) is sex, age, height, and weight.

**2.** 次の (1), (2) の写真について、それぞれの写真を説明する英文が 4 つ聞こえてきます。最も適切な英文の記号を○で囲みなさい。

(1)

(A)　　(B)　　(C)　　(D)

(2)

(A)　　(B)　　(C)　　(D)

**3.** 1.〜3. の英文につづいて、(A), (B), (C) の 3 つの応答文が聞こえます。それぞれの英文の応答文として最も適切な応答文の記号を○で囲みなさい。 🎧 T₈

1. (A)　(B)　(C)
2. (A)　(B)　(C)
3. (A)　(B)　(C)

(Exercise 4 と Exercise 5 は解答提出問題です)

**4.** 会話文を聴き、その会話に関する質問文 (1), (2) の答えとして最も適切なものを (A)〜(D) より選び、巻末解答用紙の記号を○で囲みなさい。 🎧 T₉

(1) Why hasn't the woman cleaned the living room?
　　(A) She has been cooking.
　　(B) She wasn't expecting guests.
　　(C) She wants the man to do it.
　　(D) Cleaning makes her busy.

(2) Why must the living room be cleaned?
　　(A) The woman has to make supper.
　　(B) The couple is expecting guests.
　　(C) The man did it already.
　　(D) It has never been cleaned before.

**5.** 英文を聴き、その英文に関する質問文 (3), (4) の答えとして最も適切なものを (A)〜(D) より選び、巻末解答用紙の記号を○で囲みなさい。 🎧 T₁₀

(3) Why shouldn't students wait until the end of term to decide their paper topic?
　　(A) The due date has not been settled.
　　(B) Recent papers have been the best.
　　(C) Even if they wait, they might not hit upon a good idea.
　　(D) The first weeks of class are more interesting.

(4) What is the professor's main point?
　　(A) Students should begin to think about their final paper early.
　　(B) The final paper will be due sometime at the end of the term.
　　(C) Students who don't take notes might be lost and struggle.
　　(D) Students should focus their thoughts on the first few weeks of class.

# Unit 3

# Every time I call,
# I get a busy signal.

**Points**

このユニットでは、「電話」に関する語句・表現と、「数量」に関する語句・表現を聴き取る
練習を行います。

## Section A  Telephones [電話]

### ❑ Key Words and Expressions

15

**1. Busy signal** （話し中の信号音）

Every time I call, I get a <u>busy signal</u>.

**2. Call back** （～に折り返し電話をする）

He left a message for me to <u>call</u> him <u>back</u>.

**3. Get cut off** （電話を切られる）

Each time I call their service number, I <u>get cut off</u>.

**4. Put ... on hold** （～を電話口で待たせる）

The last time I phoned his office, he <u>put</u> me <u>on hold</u> for 20 minutes.

**5. Leave a message** （メッセージを残す）

Mr. Smith wasn't in, so I <u>left a message</u> for him to call back.

**6. Take a call / Make a call** （電話に出る／電話をする）

Sorry, but I have to <u>take a call</u> on another line.

## ❏ 𝑻raining 𝑨-1:

16

音声を聴いて空所に正しい語句を書き入れなさい。

1. A: Hi, I'm Ben Taylor of Payton Industries calling for Elizabeth Martin.
   B. Ms. Martin is in a meeting now. Do you want to ( )?
   Or can I have her ( )?

2. A: I hate calling city hall. I always ( ).
   B: Right. Or they ( ).

3. A: He never ( ) during his lunch break.
   B: But I ( ) so he must be in.

## ❏ 𝑻raining 𝑨-2:

17

英文を聴き、その英文に関する質問文の答えとして最も適切なものを (A)〜(D) より選びなさい。

Question: What was most frustrating about this company's telephone service?
  (A) They went out of business.
  (B) They cut callers off.
  (C) They would not return calls.
  (D) They didn't expect success.

## Section B  Number/Quantity [数量]

## ❏ 𝑲ey 𝑾ords and 𝑬xpressions

18

1. **Amount / Number**（量：総額／数）
   The annual <u>amount</u> of snowfall is not very high.

2. **How many / How much**（どのくらいの数／どのくらいの量）
   <u>How much</u> did he weigh before his diet?

3. **Increase / Decrease**（増加、増大／減少、低下）
   The last few years have seen a gradual <u>increase</u> in the number of tourists.

4. **Low / High**（低い／高い）
   I received the <u>lowest</u> mark on the recent math test.

12

**5. More / Less** （より多くの／より少ない）

There are <u>more</u> accidents related to smartphones each year.

**6. Percent / Percentage** （パーセント、割合）

Some people arrive by train, but a higher <u>percentage</u> come by car.

## ❏ *Training B-1：*

19

音声を聴いて空所に正しい語句を書き入れなさい。

**1.** A: We receive (　　　　　　　　　) rainfall each year.
　　 B: That's why the lake has such a (　　　) water level.

**2.** A: (　　　　　　　) homes here have swimming pools?
　　 B: I'm not sure, but the (　　　　　　) is high.

**3.** A: The criminals escaped (　　　　　　　　　　　　) money.
　　 B: I think we need to (　　　　　) the number of police patrols.

## ❏ *Training B-2：*

20

会話文を聴き、その会話に関する質問文の答えとして最も適切なものを (A) ～ (D) より選びなさい。

**Question: What does the first speaker want?**
　　(A) To borrow money
　　(B) To be shorter
　　(C) A higher bill
　　(D) To know the amount

21

### ┌─ *Practice for Sound Change:* ［音変化に慣れよう］ 連 結 ③ ─

「摩擦音 [f][v][s][z][θ][ð] ＋ 母音」の音変化

1. She published <u>half of</u> her works after she turned 80.
2. Many people <u>give up</u> their New Year's resolutions in January.
3. Her <u>dress is</u> purple <u>with a</u> high collar and long sleeves.
4. She <u>has always</u> taken calls from her two daughters during work hours.
5. Williams scored <u>both of</u> his tries in the first half.

13

# Exercises

**1.** 次の (1)～(5) の英文を聴き取り、それぞれの空所に語句を書き入れなさい。 🎧 CD T 11

(1) Most phones let you (                  ) to increase the headset volume.

(2) In order to (                ), you need lots of practice.

(3) The (              ) is to increase student achievement.

(4) If you (      ) this area, you have to put up (        ) traffic noise.

(5) She called to thank me (          ) the entire staff.


**2.** 次の (1), (2) の写真について、それぞれの写真を説明する英文が 4 つ聞こえてきます。最も適切な英文の記号を◯で囲みなさい。 🎧 CD T 12

(1)

(A)   (B)   (C)   (D)

(2)

(A)   (B)   (C)   (D)

**3.** 1.～3. の英文につづいて、(A), (B), (C) の 3 つの応答文が聞こえます。それぞれの英文の応答文として最も適切な応答文の記号を○で囲みなさい。　🎧T13

1. (A)　(B)　(C)
2. (A)　(B)　(C)
3. (A)　(B)　(C)

(Exercise 4 と Exercise 5 は解答提出問題です)

**4.** 会話文を聴き、その会話に関する質問文 (1), (2) の答えとして最も適切なものを (A)～(D) より選び、巻末解答用紙の記号を○で囲みなさい。　🎧T14

(1) **Why does the woman have so many shoes?**
    (A) Her closet is large.
    (B) She collects them.
    (C) She has big feet.
    (D) She wants to surprise people.

(2) **What does the man think about the woman's closet?**
    (A) She needs one more.
    (B) She needs to increase the number.
    (C) It isn't large enough.
    (D) It needs more feet.

**5.** 英文を聴き、その英文に関する質問文 (3), (4) の答えとして最も適切なものを (A)～(D) より選び、巻末解答用紙の記号を○で囲みなさい。　🎧T15

(3) **Why are automated answering services popular?**
    (A) They help callers speak to live representatives.
    (B) They allow callers to use their keypads.
    (C) They reduce being put on hold.
    (D) They cut off calls automatically.

(4) **What happens if callers cannot complete calls with only their keypads?**
    (A) They can try an automated answering service.
    (B) They can speak to a human representative.
    (C) They may get put on hold.
    (D) They have to record a voice message.

# Unit 4

# I crammed all night
# for the history exam.

**Points**

このユニットでは、「学校」に関する語句・表現と、「感情」に関する語句・表現を聴き取る
練習を行います。

## Section A　School［学校］

### ❏ *Key Words and Expressions*

22

1. **Cram**（一夜漬けの勉強をする）

   I <u>crammed</u> all night for the history exam.

2. **Credit**（単位）

   If you have too many absences, you may not get <u>credit</u> for the course.

3. **Lecture**（講義）

   His online <u>lectures</u> are so boring. Everyone falls asleep.

4. **Notes**（メモ、ノート）

   I don't have <u>notes</u> from the last lecture because I was absent.

5. **Pass / Fail**（～に合格する／～に落ちる）

   I've got to <u>pass</u> the final exam or I might fail the course.

6. **Submit / Due**（を提出する／締め切りで）

   The paper is <u>due</u> at the end of the month, but
   students can <u>submit</u> it early.

## ❑ *Training A-1*:

23

音声を聴いて空所に正しい語句を書き入れなさい。

**1.** A: When is the homework ( )? Do you know?

　　B: No, I've been absent for the last two ( ).

**2.** A: I ( ) the exam, but I don't have any confidence.

　　B: At least you ( ). I always fall asleep in class.

**3.** A: If I don't ( ) I won't be able to graduate.

　　B: Then study hard ( ) the test.

## ❑ *Training A-2*:

24

英文を聴き、その英文に関する質問文の答えとして最も適切なものを (A)〜(D) より選びなさい。

**Question: What makes the exam easier than the paper?**

　　(A) Students can submit it one week after class.

　　(B) Students can refer to their notes.

　　(C) Students need not worry about quality.

　　(D) The research paper is the key.

## Section B　Emotions ［感情］

## ❑ *Key Words and Expressions*

25

**1. Be excited / Exciting**（(人が) ワクワクして／(人を) ワクワクさせる）

She's very <u>excited</u> about studying abroad.

**2. Impatient / Patient**（がまんできない／忍耐強い）

<u>Impatient</u> people get angry quickly.

**3. Impress / Be impressed**（〜を感動させる／感動する）

The new mayor has yet to <u>impress</u> me with his plans for the city.

**4. Be pleased / Be delighted**（満足して：うれしい／うれしい）

I'm always <u>pleased</u> with your work.

5. **Upset / Angry**（気が動転して／怒って）

My mother is very <u>upset</u> over my test scores.

6. **Be worried**（心配して）

<u>I'm</u> very <u>worried</u> about my father's health.

## ❏ *Training B-1*:

26

音声を聴いて空所に正しい語句を書き入れなさい。

1. A: I was (                    ) that you attended my recital.
   B: It was (                         ) you play! You're talented!

2. A: I am very (                    ) his attitude.
   B: Be (            ). He's only a child.

3. A: I'm (                    ) with the new highway.
   B: It's nice, but I (            ) that our taxes will go up.

## ❏ *Training B-2*:

27

会話文を聴き、その会話に関する質問文の答えとして最も適切なものを (A)〜(D) より選びなさい。

**Question: Why does the father emphasize patience?**

(A) The girl doesn't impress him.

(B) The girl is too excited.

(C) They have been dating for so long.

(D) Their son changes girlfriends often.

28

┌─ *Practice for Sound Change:* ［音変化に慣れよう］ **連 結 ④** ─┐

「その他の子音 [m; n; l; r] ＋母音」の音変化を扱います。

1. Our children <u>tell us</u> they feel safe at school.
2. The online <u>classroom is</u> available when needed.
3. Here are the reasons why students study hard but still <u>fail in</u> school.
4. Please <u>come and</u> <u>join us for an important</u> discussion on higher education.
5. Due to the decreasing <u>number of</u> shoppers, our sales target is still <u>far away</u>.

# Exercises

**1.** 次の (1)～(5) の英文を聴き取り、それぞれの空所に語句を書き入れなさい。

(1) Our teacher showed a detailed (　　　　　　　　　　) for the annual school festival.

(2) Please (　　　　　　　　　) any change in your class schedule as soon as possible.

(3) In my class, several students have advanced (　　　　　　　　　).

(4) I have no time to (　　　　　　　　　) for my marketing class, but I have to do it.

(5) It sometimes takes time for sorrow to (　　　　　) joy.

**2.** 次の (1), (2) の写真について、それぞれの写真を説明する英文が 4 つ聞こえてきます。最も適切な英文の記号を○で囲みなさい。

(1)

(A)　(B)　(C)　(D)

(2)

(A)　(B)　(C)　(D)

**3.** 1.〜3. の英文につづいて、(A), (B), (C) の 3 つの応答文が聞こえます。それぞれの英文の
応答文として最も適切な応答文の記号を○で囲みなさい。

1. (A) (B) (C)
2. (A) (B) (C)
3. (A) (B) (C)

（Exercise 4 と Exercise 5 は解答提出問題です）

**4.** 会話文を聴き、その会話に関する質問文 (1), (2) の答えとして最も適切なものを (A)〜(D)
より選び、巻末解答用紙の記号を○で囲みなさい。

(1) **What is the woman's concern?**
  (A) They failed to get tickets.
  (B) Their seats are too close.
  (C) The game is not so exciting.
  (D) Their seats are far from the playing field.

(2) **Why isn't the man worried?**
  (A) He loves the seats.
  (B) He is sure the seats are adequate.
  (C) The woman is very upset.
  (D) He likes terrible seats.

**5.** 英文を聴き、その英文に関する質問文 (3), (4) の答えとして最も適切なものを (A)〜(D) よ
り選び、巻末解答用紙の記号を○で囲みなさい。

(3) **What is most important in passing Professor Simmons' class?**
  (A) Doing all the homework
  (B) Paying attention to details
  (C) Taking notes in depth
  (D) Cramming for information

(4) **Who fails Professor Simmons' exams?**
  (A) Only a few students
  (B) Students who take detailed notes
  (C) Students who fail to submit homework
  (D) Those students with inadequate notes

# Unit 5

# The departure time has been changed due to high winds.

## Points

このユニットでは、「交通・運輸」に関する語句・表現と、「賛成・反対；同意・不同意」に関する語句・表現を聴き取る練習を行います。

## Section A Transportation [交通・運輸]

### ❏ Key Words and Expressions

29

1. **Commute (n) / Commute (v)** （通勤／通勤する）
   My <u>commute</u> is much shorter if I use public transportation.

2. **Delay / Be delayed** （遅延／遅れる）
   This train line has frequent <u>delays</u> during rush hour.

3. **Departure / Arrival** （出発／到着）
   The <u>departure</u> time has been changed due to high winds.

4. **Miss** （～に乗りそこなう）
   If I <u>miss</u> my bus, I'll be late for work.

5. **Passenger** （乗客）
   There were so many <u>passengers</u> that I couldn't find a seat.

6. **Traffic** （交通（量））
   <u>Traffic</u> is always heavy on Friday evenings.

## ❏ *Training A-1*:

30

音声を聴いて空所に正しい語句を書き入れなさい。

1. A: (                    ) is still scheduled for 9:00!
   B: I thought for sure we'd (              )!

2. A: The bus might be late (              ).
   B: Gosh. If it's too late, I'll (              ).

3. A: The train is always (                    ).
   B: That's why I prefer (            ) by car.

## ❏ *Training A-2*:

31

英文を聴き、その英文に関する質問文の答えとして最も適切なものを (A)〜(D) より選びなさい。

Question: How do train delays affect train travel?
   (A) They cause people to commute at off-peak times.
   (B) They help passengers avoid crowds.
   (C) They make travel more crowded.
   (D) They make traffic less heavy.

## Section B  Agreement/Disagreement; Approval/Disapproval
[賛成・反対；同意・不同意]

## ❏ *Key Words and Expressions*

32

1. **Be against / Be all for**（〜に反対である／〜に大賛成である）
   I <u>am against</u> raising taxes again this year.

2. **Agree with / Disagree with**（〜に賛成である／〜に反対である）
   I <u>disagree with</u> anyone who says that city life is convenient.

3. **Complain about**（〜に文句を言う、〜に不満を表す）
   She <u>complains about</u> her husband all the time.

4. **Don't mind**（気にしない）
   I <u>don't mind</u> what he said. It's his attitude I dislike.

22

5. **Don't mean to** *do*（〜するつもりではない）

I <u>didn't mean to</u> offend you when I criticized your boss.

6. **Prefer**（〜を好む）

I <u>prefer</u> not to talk about what happened.

## ❏ *Training B-1*:

33

音声を聴いて空所に正しい語句を書き入れなさい。

**1.** A: He (              ) too much.

    B: I (       ). I wish he'd stop.

**2.** A: I (            ) make you mad, but I thought I should say some-

      thing.

    B: Oh, (          ). I'm glad you're being honest.

**3.** A: I'm (         ) getting a tattoo.

    B: I'd (       ) talk about it.

## ❏ *Training B-2*:

34

会話文を聴き、その会話に関する質問文の答えとして最も適切なものを (A) 〜 (D) より選びなさい。

**Question: What do these two disagree about?**

    (A) The construction of a new city hall

    (B) Taxes going up

    (C) The timing of the new building

    (D) How to complain

35

---
**Practice for Sound Change:** ［音変化に慣れよう］ 連 結 ⑤

「子音＋[j]」の音変化を扱います。

1. A shuttle bus will <u>meet you</u> <u>at your</u> hotel and take you to the station.
2. We <u>need your</u> feedback to improve transportation in our region.
3. Traffic is busier <u>than usual</u> due to the bus drivers' strike.
4. If you don't like exercising <u>on your</u> own, this class will help you.
5. The website <u>is useful</u> for passengers when booking flights.

---

# Exercises

**1.** 次の (1)～(5) の英文を聴き取り、それぞれの空所に語句を書き入れなさい。 CD T 21

(1) "Can I (                               ) favor?" — "Sure, what is it?"

(2) I agree to (                                      ) and its fundraising drive.

(3) If you (                          ), your ticket will no longer be valid.

(4) (                              ) and others from COVID-19 (                  ) public transportation.

(5) The contract is (                                            ) to attend annual meetings.

**2.** 次の (1), (2) の写真について、それぞれの写真を説明する英文が 4 つ聞こえてきます。最も適切な英文の記号を○で囲みなさい。 CD T 22

(1)

(A)    (B)    (C)    (D)

(2)

(A)    (B)    (C)    (D)

**3.** 1.～3. の英文につづいて、(A), (B), (C) の 3 つの応答文が聞こえます。それぞれの英文の
応答文として最も適切な応答文の記号を○で囲みなさい。 CD T/23

1. (A)　(B)　(C)
2. (A)　(B)　(C)
3. (A)　(B)　(C)

（Exercise 4 と Exercise 5 は解答提出問題です）

**4.** 会話文を聴き、その会話に関する質問文 (1), (2) の答えとして最も適切なものを (A)～(D)
より選び、巻末解答用紙の記号を○で囲みなさい。 CD T/24

(1) **Why was the woman late?**
    (A) Her train was delayed.
    (B) She missed her train.
    (C) She always comes by car.
    (D) Traffic was too heavy.

(2) **What does the man suggest?**
    (A) She shouldn't be late.
    (B) She should quit coming by car.
    (C) She should avoid heavy traffic.
    (D) She should never miss her train.

**5.** 英文を聴き、その英文に関する質問文 (3), (4) の答えとして最も適切なものを (A)～(D) よ
り選び、巻末解答用紙の記号を○で囲みなさい。 CD T/25

(3) **What is this company's approach to customers who complain?**
    (A) It takes an immediate stance against them.
    (B) It is always ready to argue.
    (C) It wants customers to serve them.
    (D) It hopes to understand customer opinions.

(4) **What should service agents avoid?**
    (A) Arguing
    (B) Disagreeing
    (C) Listening
    (D) Complaining

# Unit 6

# The forecast looks good for the weekend.

===== Points =====

このユニットでは、「天候・自然」に関する語句・表現と、「評価・比較など」に関する語句・表現を聴き取る練習を行います。

## Section A  **Weather/Nature** [天候・自然]

### ❑ *Key Words and Expressions*

36

**1. At risk**（危険で）

This area is <u>at risk</u> of flooding during heavy rain.

**2. Clear / Fair**（晴れた）

The weather is typically <u>fair</u> at this time of year.

**3. Evacuate**（避難する；避難させる）

Residents should be prepared to <u>evacuate</u> if the river rises.

**4. Forecast**（天気予報；予測）

The <u>forecast</u> looks good for the weekend.

**5. Severe / Chilly**（ひどい、厳しい／冷え冷えする、肌寒い）

<u>Severe</u> weather occurs often during the hot months of summer.

**6. Storm**（あらし、暴風（雨））

The <u>storm</u> brought heavy rain all along the coast.

## ❏ *Training A-1:*
37

音声を聴いて空所に正しい語句を書き入れなさい。

1. A: I hope we have (　　　　　　　　) for the picnic.
   B: Yes, but (　　　　　　　) doesn't look very good.

2. A: I've heard this area is (　　　　　　　　) having landslides during heavy rain.
   B: Yes, at times we (　　　　　　　　) as a precaution.

3. A: That was (　　　　　　　) we had last night.
   B: The weather seems to (　　　　　　　　) every year.

## ❏ *Training A-2:*
38

会話文を聴き、その会話に関する質問文の答えとして最も適切なものを (A)〜(D) より選びなさい。

**Question: What surprised them about the storm?**
　(A) It came at night.
　(B) The severe weather was unexpected.
　(C) It caused heavy flooding.
　(D) It was on television.

## Section B　Evaluation/Judgment/Comparison

評価・比較など

## ❏ *Key Words and Expressions*
39

1. **Check for**（〜を調べる）
   When buying apples, <u>check for</u> marks on the skin.

2. **Compared to**（〜と比べると）
   <u>Compared to</u> our last car, this one has more room.

3. **Similar**（類似の、似た）
   His first two novels had very <u>similar</u> plots.

4. **Superior to / Inferior to**（〜よりも優れている／〜よりも劣っている）
   The view from here is <u>superior to</u> that of our last hotel.

**5. Than usual** （いつもより）

The coffee they served today is stronger <u>than usual</u>.

**6. Without exception** （例外なく）

Customers prefer chocolate over vanilla almost <u>without exception</u>.

## ❏ *Training B-1:*

40

音声を聴いて空所に正しい語句を書き入れなさい。

1. A: The beef and fish sets seem (                    ).
   B: Yes, but most people order the fish (                        ).

2. A: Your new apartment is (                ) your previous place.
   B: Pricier too. The rent is almost double (            ) where I lived
   before.

3. A: This melon is (                ).
   B: Oh? It might be old. (            ) discoloring.

## ❏ *Training B-2:*

41

英文を聴き、その英文に関する質問文の答えとして最も適切なものを (A)〜(D) より選びなさい。

**Question: Why does Mildred like her new hair salon better?**
   (A) It costs less.
   (B) It has better service.
   (C) The location is good.
   (D) Her new hairstyle is better.

42

### *Practice for Sound Change:* ［音変化に慣れよう］ 連 結 ⑥

「母音と母音がつながる」音変化を扱います。

1. The government plans to <u>go ahead</u> with a climate change summit at the end of the month.
2. <u>You all</u> worked so hard on your project and I'm proud of you.
3. It's a fine day for <u>do-it</u>-yourself projects around the home.
4. Does anyone have an <u>idea of</u> what this is worth?
5. We always <u>rely on</u> weather forecasts for upcoming events.

# Exercises

**1.** 次の (1)〜(5) の英文を聴き取り、それぞれの空所に語句を書き入れなさい。

(1) The healthcare system (          ) superior to that of Japan.

(2) When I (          ), I like to learn new things.

(3) We strongly suggest (          ) the sites.

(4) It's really fine today. You've (          ) right now.

(5) All farmers (          ) weather forecasts when planning their work.


**2.** 次の (1), (2) の写真について、それぞれの写真を説明する英文が 4 つ聞こえてきます。最も適切な英文の記号を○で囲みなさい。

(1)

        (A)    (B)    (C)    (D)

(2)

        (A)    (B)    (C)    (D)

**3.** 1.～3. の英文につづいて、(A), (B), (C) の 3 つの応答文が聞こえます。それぞれの英文の応答文として最も適切な応答文の記号を○で囲みなさい。

1. (A)　(B)　(C)
2. (A)　(B)　(C)
3. (A)　(B)　(C)

（Exercise 4 と Exercise 5 は解答提出問題です）

**4.** 会話文を聴き、その会話に関する質問文 (1), (2) の答えとして最も適切なものを (A)～(D) より選び、巻末解答用紙の記号を○で囲みなさい。

**(1)  How is the sister like her brother?**
　　　(A) They are both good students.
　　　(B) Neither has a proper attitude.
　　　(C) Both like to joke.
　　　(D) They are difficult to compare.

**(2)  What seems to be the sister's weak point?**
　　　(A) She is a poor student.
　　　(B) She has a superior attitude.
　　　(C) She jokes too much.
　　　(D) She is similar to her brother.

**5.** 英文を聴き、その英文に関する質問文 (3), (4) の答えとして最も適切なものを (A)～(D) より選び、巻末解答用紙の記号を○で囲みなさい。

**3.  What may cause flooding?**
　　　(A) A severe weather forecast
　　　(B) Bad weather tomorrow
　　　(C) People who live near the river
　　　(D) Heavy rain this evening

**4.  When should residents evacuate?**
　　　(A) If they live in Jefferson County
　　　(B) If the storm moves east
　　　(C) If the rainfall gets heavier
　　　(D) If the skies start to clear

# Unit 7

# They offer a ten percent discount if you pay with cash.

============================ **Points** ============================

このユニットでは、「ショッピング」に関する語句・表現と、「計画・予定」に関する語句・表現を聴き取る練習を行います。

## Section A  Shopping ［ショッピング］

### ❏ Key Words and Expressions

43

1. **Customer**（客、顧客）

   She's a regular <u>customer</u> at this shop.

2. **Deliver**（配達する；を配達する）

   They have good prices on furniture, but they don't <u>deliver</u>.

3. **Discount**（割引；を割引する）

   They offer a ten percent <u>discount</u> if you pay with cash.

4. **Merchandise**（商品）

   This store has a lot of unique <u>merchandise</u>.

5. **Sale**（安売り；販売）

   All this month they are having a <u>sale</u> on electrical appliances.

6. **Be sold out**（売り切れる）

   I tried to buy some blue cheese bagels but they <u>were sold out</u>.

## ❏ *T*raining *A-1:*

44

音声を聴いて空所に正しい語句を書き入れなさい。

1. A: I thought you (                    ) on barbecue grills.
   B: We did, but (                    ) in just two hours.

2. A: Sorry, sir, but the (                              ) with this
   (                    ).
   B: Aw, please! I'm a (                    )!

3. A: If I buy this sofa, do you (          )?
   B: Certainly, but there is a delivery fee.

## ❏ *T*raining *A-2:*

45

会話文を聴き、その会話に関する質問文の答えとして最も適切なものを (A) ～ (D) より選びなさい。

**Question: How much does the customer want to pay?**
   (A) The regular price
   (B) Half price
   (C) More than half price
   (D) Less than half price

## Section B **Planning/Scheduling** [計画・予定]

## ❏ *K*ey *W*ords and *E*xpressions

46

1. **Appointment** (予約、約束)
   I have a doctor's <u>appointment</u> next Friday afternoon.

2. **Free** (暇な、手があいて)
   I'm <u>free</u> for lunch all next week.

3. **Have time for** (～の時間がある)
   I'm so busy that I hardly <u>have time for</u> housework.

4. **Plan to** *do* (～する予定である)
   I <u>plan to</u> retire next year after my sixtieth birthday.

5. **Put off**（～を延期する）

The meeting was <u>put off</u> until next week due to the boss's illness.

6. **Be scheduled for / Schedule (n)**（～の予定である／スケジュール、予定）

The Jobs Fair <u>is scheduled for</u> the end of the month.

## ❑ *Training B-1* :

47

音声を聴いて空所に正しい語句を書き入れなさい。

1. A:  Are you (　　　　　　　) tennis this weekend?
   B:  Sorry, I (　　　　　　　　　).

2. A:  Why don't you skip your (　　　　　　　　　　　) and come to lunch?
   B:  No, I can't (　　　　　　　) any longer.

3. A:  The (　　　　　　　　　　　　) for the first week in July.
   B:  I know. I (　　　　　　) attend.

## ❑ *Training B-2* :

48

英文を聴き、その英文に関する質問文の答えとして最も適切なものを (A) ～ (D) より選びなさい。

**Question: What does the speaker wish to know?**
   (A)  About what happened at the presentation
   (B)  About his dental appointment
   (C)  About his routine check-up
   (D)  About what he had forgotten

49

─ *Practice for Sound Change:* [音変化に慣れよう] 脱落①─

「破裂音 [p, b; t, d; k, g] ＋破裂音 [p, b; t, d; k, g]」の音変化を扱います。

1. The council agreed to <u>develop plans</u> to build a new city hall.
2. <u>Take care</u> <u>not to</u> become infected, even if your COVID-19 vaccine is coming soon.
3. Aren't you <u>supposed to</u> be here by 8:00? You arrived <u>late twice</u> this week!
4. New employees will receive <u>job training</u> at this store.
5. October through December is a <u>good time</u> to buy a <u>used car</u>.

# Exercises

**1.** 次の (1)〜(5) の英文を聴き取り、それぞれの空所に語句を書き入れなさい。

(1) Can you (             ) the supermarket and get some milk?

(2) When I go shopping, I always ask "Do you (             ) senior citizens?"

(3) Here are six ways you can (             ) your schedule.

(4) The company (             ) textile plant that would employ 600 people.

(5) CNN has taken a (             ) on global warming.

**2.** 次の (1), (2) の写真について、それぞれの写真を説明する英文が 4 つ聞こえてきます。最も適切な英文の記号を○で囲みなさい。

(1)

(A)     (B)     (C)     (D)

(2)

(A)     (B)     (C)     (D)

**3.** 1.～3. の英文につづいて、(A), (B), (C) の 3 つの応答文が聞こえます。それぞれの英文の
応答文として最も適切な応答文の記号を○で囲みなさい。

**1.** (A)　(B)　(C)
**2.** (A)　(B)　(C)
**3.** (A)　(B)　(C)

(Exercise 4 と Exercise 5 は解答提出問題です)

**4.** 会話文を聴き、その会話に関する質問文 (1), (2) の答えとして最も適切なものを (A)～(D)
より選び、巻末解答用紙の記号を○で囲みなさい。

(1) What does the man hope to purchase?
　　(A) Something not on discount
　　(B) Golf merchandise
　　(C) The ad doesn't say.
　　(D) Ten items on discount

(2) How much money will the man save?
　　(A) Ten percent if he purchases goods during the sale
　　(B) Ten percent if he buys all items
　　(C) Ten percent if he brings the ad
　　(D) Ten percent if he buys only golf equipment

**5.** 英文を聴き、その英文に関する質問文 (3), (4) の答えとして最も適切なものを (A)～(D) よ
り選び、巻末解答用紙の記号を○で囲みなさい。

(3) Why is the fair being held in late July?
　　(A) The products can arrive from overseas.
　　(B) Prices are more reasonable then.
　　(C) It had to be put off for a few weeks.
　　(D) No one was free till that time.

(4) What does the speaker recommend people do at the fair?
　　(A) Attend during the last week of July
　　(B) Try international food
　　(C) Avoid severe weather
　　(D) Leave family members at home

# Unit 8

# I didn't hear the outcome of the game.

**Points**

このユニットでは、「スポーツ」に関する語句・表現と、「情報のやりとり」に関する語句・表現を聴き取る練習を行います。

## Section A  Sports [スポーツ]

### ❑ *Key Words and Expressions*

50

1. **Career**（職業；職歴）

   After a twenty-year <u>career</u> as a player, he had an even longer <u>career</u> as a sports announcer.

2. **Expectations**（期待）

   <u>Expectations</u> are high for City College basketball this year.

3. **Miss**（を打ちそこなう；を逃す）

   He <u>missed</u> an open shot at the goal.

4. **Outcome**（結果）

   I didn't hear the <u>outcome</u> of the game.

5. **Round**（（スポーツの）1回、ラウンド）

   We lost in the very first <u>round</u> of the tournament.

6. **Favorite** (n/adj)（本命、優勝候補；好きな）

   I always cheer for the <u>favorite</u>.

36

## ❏ *Training A-1*:

51

音声を聴いて空所に正しい語句を書き入れなさい。

1. A:  I heard your team lost in (                           ).
   B:  Yeah, I just (                    ) at the last second.

2. A:  I heard (                    ) weren't so high when you started out.
   B:  No, I was a little short and slow. But I ended up (                    ).

3. A:  The other team is a big (                ), so I imagine we'll lose.
   B:  Who cares about (                ). Let's just play hard.

## ❏ *Training A-2*:

52

会話文を聴き、その会話に関する質問文の答えとして最も適切なものを (A) 〜 (D) より選びなさい。

Question: According to the interviewed player, who will win the tournament?
   (A)  The favorite
   (B)  City College
   (C)  His team
   (D)  The expected team

## Section B  Exchange Information [情報のやりとり]

## ❏ *Key Words and Expressions*

53

1. **Brainstorm** （ブレインストーミングする）
   We spent the entire meeting <u>brainstorming</u> for ideas.

2. **Comment on** （〜について批評 [コメント] する）
   He was reluctant to <u>comment on</u> the trade dispute.

3. **Discuss** （〜について話し合う）
   At the meeting, we <u>discussed</u> ways to increase sales.

4. **Explain** （〜を説明する）
   I asked her to <u>explain</u> the process one more time.

5. Inquire into（〜を調査する）

I <u>inquired into</u> rental costs in that apartment building.

6. Remind（〜に思い出させる）

I had to <u>remind</u> him of the date of the meeting.

## ❏ *Training B-1:*

54

音声を聴いて空所に正しい語句を書き入れなさい。

1. A: First, (               ) my understanding of the agreement.
   B: Okay. I'll (       ) when you're finished.

2. A: Did you (        ) rental properties?
   B: No, I forgot. (        ) to do it tomorrow.

3. A: Yesterday we (          ) ideas for sales promotions.
   B: Tell me your top suggestions and we can (      ).

## ❏ *Training B-2:*

55

英文を聴き、その英文に関する質問文の答えとして最も適切なものを (A)〜(D) より選びなさい。

Question: According to this passage, what is most important for successful writing?
   (A) Contacting the instructor
   (B) Brainstorming
   (C) Selecting a good topic
   (D) Attending the first week of class

56

---
### *Practice for Sound Change:* [音変化に慣れよう] 脱 落 ②

「破裂音 [p, b; t, d; k, g]＋摩擦音 [f][v][s][z][θ][ð]」 中心の音変化を扱います。

1. I used to <u>sit there</u> when I was a child.
2. The <u>first floor</u> is the shopping area, and the <u>top floor</u> is a storage space.
3. One suspect was wearing a <u>black shirt</u>; the other was wearing a blue shirt.
4. These cars are of <u>great value</u> to fans of the era of classic models.
5. In the morning, the <u>first thing</u> she does is to jog <u>around the</u> neighborhood.
---

# Exercises

**1.** 次の (1)〜(5) の英文を聴き取り、それぞれの空所に語句を書き入れなさい。

(1) Today's theme is "Is the world (　　　　　　　　　) environmental disaster?"

(2) To answer that question, I'd like to repeat a (　　　　　　　　　) one of last year's participants.

(3) I sent my children mail to (　　　　　　　　　) Mother's day.

(4) Many workplace skills only (　　　　　　　　　) extensive experience.

(5) The steakhouse is something of a (　　　　　　　　　) sports fans and athletes in Vancouver.

**2.** 次の (1), (2) の写真について、それぞれの写真を説明する英文が 4 つ聞こえてきます。最も適切な英文の記号を○で囲みなさい。

(1)　　　　　　　　　　　　　　　(2)

(1)　　(A)　　(B)　　(C)　　(D)　　　　　　(2)　　(A)　　(B)　　(C)　　(D)

3. 1.～3. の英文につづいて、(A), (B), (C) の 3 つの応答文が聞こえます。それぞれの英文の応答文として最も適切な応答文の記号を○で囲みなさい。 🔊T38

1. (A)　(B)　(C)
2. (A)　(B)　(C)
3. (A)　(B)　(C)


（Exercise 4 と Exercise 5 は解答提出問題です）

**4.** 会話文を聴き、その会話に関する質問文 (1), (2) の答えとして最も適切なものを (A)～(D) より選び、巻末解答用紙の記号を○で囲みなさい。 🔊T39

(1) What is the woman selling?
   (A) Advertisements
   (B) Inquiries
   (C) A newspaper
   (D) Books

(2) What does the man want her to explain?
   (A) Her advertisement
   (B) The condition of the books
   (C) The condition of the newspaper
   (D) How many ads she has


**5.** 英文を聴き、その英文に関する質問文 (3), (4) の答えとして最も適切なものを (A)～(D) より選び、巻末解答用紙の記号を○で囲みなさい。 🔊T40

(3) What ended Tom Davis' boxing career?
   (A) He lost the championship fight.
   (B) He hurt his knee.
   (C) He lost almost every fight.
   (D) No one knows the outcome.

(4) Why wasn't he favored to win?
   (A) He had a knee injury.
   (B) No one thought much of his ability.
   (C) He didn't win the championship.
   (D) He had low expectations.

# Unit 9

# I wish I had the recipe for this stew!

**Points**

このユニットでは、「レストラン・食事」に関する語句・表現と、「方法・手段」に関する語句・表現を聴き取る練習を行います。

## Section A Restaurants/Dining [レストラン・食事]

### ❏ *Key Words and Expressions*

57

1. **Choice** （選択の種類［範囲］）

   All main dishes come with a <u>choice</u> of salad or soup.

2. **Order** （注文する；〜を注文する）

   Are you ready to <u>order</u> now?

3. **Recipe** （調理法、レシピ）

   I wish I had the <u>recipe</u> for this stew!

4. **Recommend** （を薦める）

   Everything is tasty, but I'd like to <u>recommend</u> the fish course.

5. **Reserve / Reservation** （を予約する／予約）

   I <u>reserved</u> a table for eight for six o'clock.

6. **Selection** （えりすぐりの品）

   They have a large <u>selection</u> of salads.

41

## ❏ *Training A-1*:

58

音声を聴いて空所に正しい語句を書き入れなさい。

1. A: The (                          ) I could make was at nine o'clock.
   B: That's late. By the time (                  ), it will be nine-thirty.

2. A: For dessert, you (                    ) of any of our various pies or cakes.
   B: What do you (              )? The (                ) too big!

3. A: What's in the pilaf? It's so yummy.
   B: Sorry, we don't give away (                ).

## ❏ *Training A-2*:

59

英文を聴き、その英文に関する質問文の答えとして最も適切なものを (A) ～ (D) より選びなさい。

Question: What seems to make this restaurant so popular?
   (A) Everyone needs a reservation.
   (B) They serve Italian food.
   (C) It's always packed.
   (D) They offer a tremendous menu.

## Section B  Ways/Means [方法・手段]

## ❏ *Key Words and Expressions*

60

1. **Approach** (n/v) （取り組み方、方法／～に近づく）
   The best <u>approach</u> to writing a paper is to make an outline first.

2. **Handle** （を取り扱う）
   Be careful how you <u>handle</u> that saw. It's dangerous.

3. **Prepare** （を整える、を準備する）
   Before you start painting, you should first <u>prepare</u> the surface.

4. **Operate** （を操作する）
   I find old-style manual transmissions difficult to <u>operate</u>.

**5. Set up**（をセットアップする、をセットする）

I want a computer with an operating system that's easy to <u>set up</u>.

**6. Way / Method**（方法、やり方）

The <u>way</u> this bread maker works is amazing.

## ❏ *Training B-1:*

61

音声を聴いて空所に正しい語句を書き入れなさい。

**1.** A: I'm not good at (　　　　　　　) tax forms.

　　B: The (　　　　　　　　　) to have someone do them for you.

**2.** A: I can't (　　　　　) a chain saw.

　　B: But this one is simple. Even a child can (　　　　　) it.

**3.** A: I like (　　　　　) this printer works.

　　B: But it looks (　　　　　　　).

## ❏ *Training B-2:*

62

会話文を聴き、その会話に関する質問文の答えとして最も適切なものを (A)〜(D) より選びなさい。

Question: What problem does the man have with the touch pad?

　　(A) He dislikes the mouse.

　　(B) He doesn't like to play with it.

　　(C) There is nothing easier to operate.

　　(D) He isn't used to it.

63

─── *Practice for Sound Change:* ［音変化に慣れよう］　脱　落 ③ ───

「破裂音 [p, b; t, d; k, g] ＋その他の子音」の音変化を扱います。

1. The Grand Hotel features a rotating restaurant on the <u>top level</u>.
2. Fish curry with <u>coconut milk</u> makes a simple yet satisfying meal.
3. Floating your company on the <u>stock market</u> is a complex process.
4. If you want to <u>attend live</u> classes and workshops, sign up <u>right now</u>.
5. I <u>just now</u> realized I've been calling you by the wrong name all semester.

# Exercises

**1.** 次の (1)〜(5) の英文を聴き取り、それぞれの空所に語句を書き入れなさい。

(1) My (                              ) breakfast. I like to eat bacon and eggs.

(2) You can use your (                                  ) to set up your account.

(3) Roasting is (                              ) for cooking this meat.

(4) The mayor said (                          ) marked along some smaller roads.

(5) United Airlines is going to (                        ) 40 weekly flights when
England re-opens to U.S. travelers.

**2.** 次の (1), (2) の写真について、それぞれの写真を説明する英文が 4 つ聞こえてきます。
最も適切な英文の記号を○で囲みなさい。

(1)

(A)    (B)    (C)    (D)

(2)

(A)    (B)    (C)    (D)

44

**3.** 1.～3. の英文につづいて、(A), (B), (C) の 3 つの応答文が聞こえます。それぞれの英文の
応答文として最も適切な応答文の記号を○で囲みなさい。　CD T43

1. (A)　(B)　(C)
2. (A)　(B)　(C)
3. (A)　(B)　(C)

（Exercise 4 と Exercise 5 は解答提出問題です）

**4.** 会話文を聴き、その会話に関する質問文 (1), (2) の答えとして最も適切なものを (A)～(D)
より選び、巻末解答用紙の記号を○で囲みなさい。　CD T44

(1) What does the man regret?
　　(A) Coming to this restaurant
　　(B) His choice of soup
　　(C) The number of choices he had
　　(D) That he doesn't have the recipe

(2) What perhaps led to the man's problem?
　　(A) His wife's soup selection wasn't good.
　　(B) There were too many choices.
　　(C) He didn't order soup.
　　(D) He made a poor choice.

**5.** 英文を聴き、その英文に関する質問文 (3), (4) の答えとして最も適切なものを (A)～(D) よ
り選び、巻末解答用紙の記号を○で囲みなさい。　CD T45

(3) Why should painting begin on the second day?
　　(A) The paint needs to be well stirred.
　　(B) The paint must be handled carefully.
　　(C) The surface needs time to dry.
　　(D) This ensures consistency in coloring.

(4) What helps make the color consistent?
　　(A) Cleaning the surface thoroughly
　　(B) Stirring each can of paint
　　(C) Allowing time for the surface to dry
　　(D) To paint in only five minutes

# Unit 10

# Domestic and international flights have different arrival gates.

**Points**

このユニットでは、「空港・フライト」に関する語句・表現と、「原因・結果；目的・理由；場合」に関する語句・表現を聴き取る練習を行います。

## Section A Airport/Flight ［空港・フライト］

### ❑ *Key Words and Expressions*
64

1. **Aisle / Window**（通路側／窓側）
   I always try to reserve an <u>aisle</u> seat.

2. **Carry-on**（機内持ち込み手荷物）
   Your <u>carry-on</u> should be small enough to fit under the seat in front of you.

3. **Check in / Check-in**（チェックインする／チェックイン）
   You should try to <u>check in</u> early to avoid waiting in line.

4. **Delay / Cancel**（〜を遅らせる／〜をキャンセルする）
   A: Our flight has been <u>delayed</u>.
   B: I hope they don't <u>cancel</u> it.

5. **International / Domestic**（国際間の／国内の）
   <u>Domestic</u> and <u>international</u> flights have different arrival gates.

6. **Safety Regulations**（保安規定）
   Due to <u>safety regulations</u>, passengers can no longer take bottled drinks on board.

46

## ❏ *Training A-1*:

65

音声を聴いて空所に正しい語句を書き入れなさい。

1. A: With (             ) it is easier to move around.
   B: I'll ask for one (        ).

2. A: (             ) allow toothpaste of 3.4 ounces or less.
   B: I know. I put some in (       ) already.

3. A: If (       ) connection (       ), I might not make my
   (        ).
   B: Let's hope the storm passes quickly.

## ❏ *Training A-2*:

66

英文を聴き、その英文に関する質問文の答えとして最も適切なものを (A)〜(D) より選びなさい。

**Question: What makes this check-in convenient?**
   (A) It is not affected by delays or cancellations.
   (B) It covers only the domestic section of the trip.
   (C) It checks carry-ons.
   (D) It handles the entire journey.

## Section B   Cause/Effect; Purpose/Reason; Occasion

[原因・結果；目的・理由；場合]

## ❏ *Key Words and Expressions*

67

1. **Due to** （〜のために、〜のせいで）
   Our flight has been cancelled <u>due to</u> the storm.

2. **Eventually** （結局、最終的に）
   I found the seat uncomfortable, but I <u>eventually</u> fell asleep.

3. **For some reason** （どういうわけか、なぜか）
   <u>For some reason</u>, I often run into friends at the airport.

4. **How come ...?** （なぜ…？）
   <u>How come</u> that section got their meal served first?

47

**5. In case …**（…の場合には）

I always carry medicine <u>in case</u> I get sick.

**6. In order to *do***（〜するために）

I only take a carry-on <u>in order to</u> leave the airport faster.

## ❑ *Training B-1*：

68

音声を聴いて空所に正しい語句を書き入れなさい。

1. A: (                ) turbulence, I sometimes get sick on flights.
   B: (                     ), turbulence never bothers me.

2. A: (                        ) ask for an aisle seat?
   B: (                     ) use the toilet. I don't want to disturb anyone.

3. A: (                        ), you have to pass the required courses.
   B: And I will, (                ). I don't want to rush through college like everyone else.

## ❑ *Training B-2*：

69

会話文を聴き、その会話に関する質問文の答えとして最も適切なものを (A)〜(D) より選びなさい。

**Question: Why has the flight been delayed?**

(A) The reason hasn't been said.

(B) It must be due to the storm.

(C) There are too many flights.

(D) They are waiting for people to board.

70

---
**Practice for Sound Change:** [音変化に慣れよう]   脱 落 ④

「子音 +[h] で [h] 音が落ちる」音変化と「[m], [d], [g] 音が落ちる」音変化を扱います。

1. Many lives <u>could have</u> been saved if we had received vaccines earlier.
2. After listening to his message, she decided not to <u>call him</u> back.
3. You <u>should have</u> cancelled the flight so we could make other arrangements.
4. Without support <u>from my</u> father, I could not have graduated from university.
5. I'm sure he will do a <u>good job</u> this time.

---

# Exercises

**1.** 次の (1) ～ (5) の英文を聴き取り、それぞれの空所に語句を書き入れなさい。

(1) She began (　　　　　　　　　　　　) and eventually gave birth to three children.

(2) We (　　　　　　　　　　　　) to get to the airport on time.

(3) I'm calling to (　　　　　　　　　　　　) Paris this afternoon at 5:30.

(4) Passengers usually (　　　　　　　　　　　　) per hour of flight.

(5) The photo shows my grandfather (　　　　　　　　　　　　) standing in an airport queue.

**2.** 次の (1), (2) の写真について、それぞれの写真を説明する英文が 4 つ聞こえてきます。最も適切な英文の記号を○で囲みなさい。

(1)

(A)　(B)　(C)　(D)

(2)

(A)　(B)　(C)　(D)

**3.** 1.～3. の英文につづいて、(A), (B), (C) の 3 つの応答文が聞こえます。それぞれの英文の応答文として最も適切な応答文の記号を○で囲みなさい。 🎧 T48

1. (A)　(B)　(C)
2. (A)　(B)　(C)
3. (A)　(B)　(C)

(Exercise 4 と Exercise 5 は解答提出問題です)

**4.** 会話文を聴き、その会話に関する質問文 (1), (2) の答えとして最も適切なものを (A)～(D) より選び、巻末解答用紙の記号を○で囲みなさい。 🎧 T49

(1) Why does the man want the woman to answer the phone?
　　(A) He doesn't want to talk to anyone.
　　(B) He doesn't mind answering.
　　(C) He'll be busy.
　　(D) He'll be away all morning.

(2) To whom will the man be speaking?
　　(A) To his wife
　　(B) To his students
　　(C) To his teacher
　　(D) To the person on the phone

**5.** 英文を聴き、その英文に関する質問文 (3), (4) の答えとして最も適切なものを (A)～(D) より選び、巻末解答用紙の記号を○で囲みなさい。 🎧 T50

(3) How can transferring passengers learn their international flight gate numbers?
　　(A) They should walk to their new flight.
　　(B) They should wait ten to fifteen minutes.
　　(C) They should check in once more.
　　(D) They should check monitors in the corridor.

(4) What should passengers do if they cannot walk the length of the corridor?
　　(A) They should seek help from airport personnel.
　　(B) They should check monitors in the corridor.
　　(C) They should bring their carry-ons with them.
　　(D) They should proceed to their gates directly.

# Unit 11

# My operating system has an update that I need to install.

**Points**

このユニットでは、「インターネット・IT」に関する語句・表現と、「依頼・命令・要求」に関する語句・表現を聴き取る練習を行います。

## Section A  Internet/IT [インターネット・IT]

### ❑ *Key Words and Expressions*

71

1. **Attached file**（添付ファイル）
   I have included a photo of the damage in the <u>attached file</u>.

2. **Click on**（～をクリックする）
   To find the status of your package, <u>click on</u> the link to your account.

3. **Connection**（接続）
   My Internet <u>connection</u> keeps fading in and out.

4. **Enter**（～を入力する）
   To view the website, you must first <u>enter</u> your user name and password.

5. **Install**（～をインストールする）
   My operating system has an update that I need to <u>install</u>.

6. **Upload / Download**（～をアップロードする／～をダウンロードする）
   Anyone can <u>download</u> content, but only registered members can participate in chats.

51

## ❑ *Training A-1*:

72

音声を聴いて空所に正しい語句を書き入れなさい。

1. A: I don't know why my (               ) is so bad.
   B: I know a website that can help with that. (        ) this link.

2. A: I (         ) the application, but (         ).
   B: Don't look at me! I'm terrible with technology!

3. A: You can't view (           ) until you log on.
   B: I know. I (       ) my user name, but can't recall my password.

## ❑ *Training A-2*:

73

会話文を聴き、その会話に関する質問文の答えとして最も適切なものを (A)〜(D) より選びなさい。

Question: What is the first speaker's problem?
- (A) He doesn't know what is wrong.
- (B) The application is slow to install.
- (C) His Internet connection is really slow.
- (D) He can't download the application.

## Section B Offering/Ordering/Demanding

[依頼・命令・要求]

## ❑ *Key Words and Expressions*

74

1. **Ask a favor**（お願いをする、頼みごとをする）
   Can I <u>ask a favor</u> in regards to the deadline?

2. **Be invited to**（〜を要請される）
   I <u>was invited to</u> speak before the alumni association.

3. **Don't forget to** *do*（必ず〜する）
   <u>Don't forget to</u> bring in the laundry if it rains.

4. **How about …?**（〜しませんか？、〜はいかがですか？）
   <u>How about</u> joining us for lunch?

5. **Suggest**（〜を勧める、〜を提案する）

I <u>suggest</u> closing the application and restarting.

6. **Why don't you ...?**（〜しませんか？、〜したらどう？）

If you hate your job that much, <u>why don't you</u> quit?

## ❏ *Training B-1:*

75

音声を聴いて空所に正しい語句を書き入れなさい。

1. A: (　　　　　　　　　) phone his office tomorrow.
   B: (　　　　　　　　　　) instead? You know him better than I do.

2. A: I plan to (　　　　　　　　　).
   B: I (　　　　　　　　　) until after dinner. He'll be more relaxed then.

3. A: (　　　　　　　　　　) for a drink?
   B: Sorry. I (　　　　　　　　) the Hamiltons' for dinner.

## ❏ *Training B-2:*

76

英文を聴き、その英文に関する質問文の答えとして最も適切なものを (A) 〜 (D) より選びなさい。

**Question: What is the favor the man is asking?**

   (A) He wants someone to eat pizza
   (B) He wants someone to take care of his dog.
   (C) He wants someone to visit his in-laws.
   (D) He wants someone to feed his mother-in-law.

77

## *Practice for Sound Change:* [音変化に慣れよう]　脱　落 ⑤

「破裂音が文や句の最後に来るとき」の音変化を扱います。

1. Hurry <u>up</u>! The bus is at the bus <u>stop</u>.
2. Why don't you come on <u>foot</u>? You'll enjoy a great view along the way.
3. My instructors are good at emailing <u>back</u> and answering my questions.
4. "Have you got your order?" — "Not <u>yet</u>."
5. Can you come to my house <u>tonight</u>?

# Exercises

**1.** 次の (1)〜(5) の英文を聴き取り、それぞれの空所に語句を書き入れなさい。

(1) I ordered a (                    ) and I'm going to install it tomorrow.
(2) How about sending someone to greet them (                    )?
(3) Anything might happen if you click on (                    ).
(4) This will send an invitation to all users who haven't (                    ).
(5) The other day, I dropped my smartphone (                    ).

**2.** 次の (1), (2) の写真について、それぞれの写真を説明する英文が 4 つ聞こえてきます。
最も適切な英文の記号を○で囲みなさい。

(1)

(A)　　(B)　　(C)　　(D)

(2)

(A)　　(B)　　(C)　　(D)

**3.** 1.～3. の英文につづいて、(A), (B), (C) の 3 つの応答文が聞こえます。それぞれの英文の応答文として最も適切な応答文の記号を○で囲みなさい。　CD T/53

**1.** (A)　(B)　(C)
**2.** (A)　(B)　(C)
**3.** (A)　(B)　(C)


（Exercise 4 と Exercise 5 は解答提出問題です）

**4.** 会話文を聴き、その会話に関する質問文 (1), (2) の答えとして最も適切なものを (A)～(D) より選び、巻末解答用紙の記号を○で囲みなさい。　CD T/54

**(1) Why can't the woman open the attached file?**
　(A) She hasn't downloaded it yet.
　(B) She has to install the file.
　(C) She doesn't have the proper software.
　(D) She is not online.

**(2) What does the man suggest that the woman do?**
　(A) She should open the attached a file.
　(B) She should download the file first.
　(C) She should open the application in advance.
　(D) She should first install the proper application.


**5.** 英文を聴き、その英文に関する質問文 (3), (4) の答えとして最も適切なものを (A)～(D) より選び、巻末解答用紙の記号を○で囲みなさい。　CD T/55

**(3) In general, what has this part of the presentation been about?**
　(A) How to install a computer's operating system
　(B) How to find proper documentation materials
　(C) How to plug in the computer
　(D) How to fill out a required survey

**(4) According to this talk, what simple step do many people neglect doing?**
　(A) Plugging in their machine
　(B) Reading the documentation first
　(C) Installing their operating system
　(D) Viewing installation steps online

# Unit 12

# He has over a million followers on his YouTube channel.

## Points

このユニットでは、「ソーシャルライフ・SNS」に関する語句・表現と、「義務・必要」に関する語句・表現を聴き取る練習を行います。

## Section A Social Life/SNS [ソーシャルライフ・SNS]

### ❑ *Key Words and Expressions*

78

1. Chat（チャットする）

   I got into a long Internet <u>chat</u> with an old high school friend.

2. Follower（フォロワー）

   He has over a million <u>followers</u> on his YouTube channel.

3. Invite（招待する）

   I was <u>invited</u> to follow a page dedicated to my favorite soccer team.

4. Like / Share / Views（いいね／シェア／（画像・データの）表示）

   The video of his cat meowing got over one thousand <u>likes</u>.

5. Post（を投稿する、を載せる）

   I <u>posted</u> photos of my grandmother's birthday party on my Facebook page.

6. Text message（スマホのメッセージ）

   She never calls me, but sometimes she sends
   a <u>text message</u>.

56

## ❏ *Training A-1:*

79

音声を聴いて空所に正しい語句を書き入れなさい。

**1.** A: Did you (　　　　　　　　　　　) of your daughter playing in the rain?

 B: Yeah, I did. It got over (　　　　　　　　　).

**2.** A: A friend (　　　　　　　　) his page on rock music. There's a bunch of interesting chatrooms.

 B: Did you enter one? What did you (　　　　　　)?

**3.** A: I (　　　　　　　　　　) from Rebecca Moore!

 B: You're kidding! I (　　　　　　) YouTube channel!

## ❏ *Training A-2:*

80

英文を聴き、その英文に関する質問文の答えとして最も適切なものを (A)〜(D) より選びなさい。

**Question: What does the speaker invite viewers to do?**

 (A) Share her post

 (B) Follow her page

 (C) Call her false

 (D) Join her in chat

## Section B **Duty/Necessity** [義務・必要]

## ❏ *Key Words and Expressions*

81

**1. Be assigned to**（〜に配属される）

 Jane was <u>assigned to</u> the Los Angeles branch office this year.

**2. Call for**（〜を要請する、〜を要求する）

 The mayor is <u>calling for</u> peace in his quarrel with the media.

**3. In charge of**（〜の責任者で）

 His wife is <u>in charge of</u> company personnel.

**4. Ought to *do***（〜しなければならない）

 The city <u>ought to</u> place more street lamps on this road.

5. **Responsible for**（〜の責任者で）

He is <u>responsible for</u> public relations.

6. **Serve as**（〜として働く）

He <u>served as</u> class president in high school.

## ❏ *Training B-1*:

82

音声を聴いて空所に正しい語句を書き入れなさい。

**1.** A: Are you ( )?
   B: I used to be, but I was ( ) the accounting office.

**2.** A: The governor ( ) a new election.
   B: I agree. Such an action would ( ) for the future.

**3.** A: My department is ( ) local highways clean.
   B: That ( ) everyone's responsibility, not just the government's.

## ❏ *Training B-2*:

83

会話文を聴き、その会話に関する質問文の答えとして最も適切なものを (A)〜(D) より選びなさい。

**Question: What does the caller want?**
   (A) Someone else in charge of advertisements
   (B) For advertisements to be easier to see
   (C) Better glasses
   (D) More responsibility in advertising

84

┌─ *Practice for Sound Change:* [音変化に慣れよう] ⬤ 同 化 ⬤ ─┐

「前後の音が影響し合って別の音に変化する」音変化を扱います。

1. "I <u>miss you</u> all the time," he said to her as they walked along the street.
2. This website <u>gives you</u> five tips to help <u>get your</u> message across.
3. I <u>missed you</u> at the party last night.
4. You may need to <u>adjust your</u> assignment due dates.
5. We <u>need your</u> donations in order to save lives in emergencies.

# Exercises

**1.** 次の (1) 〜 (5) の英文を聴き取り、それぞれの空所に語句を書き入れなさい。　CD T/56

(1) I would like to (　　　　　　　　　　　　　　　　) meeting.

(2) An attendant will greet you (　　　　　　　　　　　) the reception hall.

(3) You can see who (　　　　　　　　　　　　　) posts through your timeline.

(4) (　　　　　　　　　　) an online job where you can work remotely.

(5) I'm calling to say (　　　　　　　　　　　) at the party.


**2.** 次の (1), (2) の写真について、それぞれの写真を説明する英文が 4 つ聞こえてきます。
最も適切な英文の記号を○で囲みなさい。　CD T/57

**(1)**

(A)　　(B)　　(C)　　(D)

**(2)**

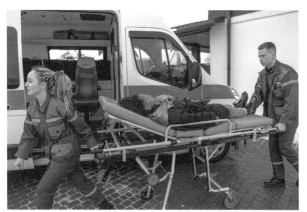

(A)　　(B)　　(C)　　(D)

**3.** 1.～3. の英文につづいて、(A), (B), (C) の 3 つの応答文が聞こえます。それぞれの英文の応答文として最も適切な応答文の記号を○で囲みなさい。 CD T 58

1. (A)　(B)　(C)
2. (A)　(B)　(C)
3. (A)　(B)　(C)

（Exercise 4 と Exercise 5 は解答提出問題です）

**4.** 会話文を聴き、その会話に関する質問文 (1), (2) の答えとして最も適切なものを (A) ～ (D) より選び、巻末解答用紙の記号を○で囲みなさい。 CD T 59

(1) What does the woman wish to complain about?
    (A) The lack of responsibility at city hall
    (B) Her friend's cousin
    (C) The road condition
    (D) Public welfare

(2) What does the man's cousin do?
    (A) He leads the Public Welfare Department at city hall.
    (B) He repairs roads.
    (C) He is responsible for city hall.
    (D) He speaks to citizens about road conditions.

**5.** 英文を聴き、その英文に関する質問文 (3), (4) の答えとして最も適切なものを (A) ～ (D) より選び、巻末解答用紙の記号を○で囲みなさい。 CD T 60

(3) How does a video go viral?
    (A) If companies buy advertisements
    (B) If many people share it
    (C) If users keep posting good content
    (D) If every poster dreams of it

(4) How many followers are desirable?
    (A) It depends on advertisements.
    (B) Only as many as the pressure allows.
    (C) It's enough to go viral.
    (D) As many followers as possible are.

# Unit 13

# She gave one of the best performances of her career.

**Points**

このユニットでは、「芸術・エンターテインメント」に関する語句・表現と、「可能・困難など」に関する語句・表現を聴き取る練習を行います。

## Section A Art/Entertainment [芸術・エンターテインメント]

### ❏ Key Words and Expressions

85

1. **Audience** (聴衆、観客)

   The <u>audience</u> applauded for over five minutes.

2. **Appeal to** (〜に受ける、〜にアピールする)

   The film <u>appeals to</u> children, but not adults.

3. **Critic** (評論家)

   Filmgoers didn't care for the movie, but <u>critics</u> loved it.

4. **Live** (ライブの、生の)

   Most programs are not <u>live</u> but recorded.

5. **Performance** (演技、演奏)

   She gave one of the best <u>performances</u> of her career.

6. **Release** (をリリースする、を公開する)

   The film will be <u>released</u> next April.

## ❏ *Training A-1:*

86

音声を聴いて空所に正しい語句を書き入れなさい。

**1.** A: (                                   ) glowing comments about his latest film.

   B: When will it (                    )? I can't wait to see it.


**2.** A: I saw him (                    ) at the state fair.

   B: How was it? I've heard his (                              ) aren't so good.


**3.** A: I didn't care for that movie at all.

   B: They say (                ) to a (                        ).


## ❏ *Training A-2:*

87

会話文を聴き、その会話に関する質問文の答えとして最も適切なものを (A) 〜 (D) より選びなさい。

**Question: Why is the first speaker depressed?**

   (A) He worries what critics will say.

   (B) The audience didn't like his performance.

   (C) He is too old to perform anymore.

   (D) He hates live performances.


## Section B  Capability/Problems/Difficulty

［可能・困難など］

## ❏ *Key Words and Expressions*

88

**1. Can't afford to *do*** （〜する余裕がない）

   If you want to reserve a seat, you <u>can't afford to</u> wait.


**2. Allow** （〜を許す）

   Pets are not <u>allowed</u> at this hotel.


**3. Available** （使う［買う、手に入れる］ことができる）

   There are no non-smoking rooms <u>available</u>.

**4. Manage to *do*** （〜をやり遂げる）

   He <u>managed to</u> graduate in only three years.

## 5. Opportunity（機会）

She has an <u>opportunity</u> to study abroad next year.

## 6. Permit / permission（を許可する／許可）

We were given <u>permission</u> to use the pool after hours.

## ❏ *Training B-1*:

89

音声を聴いて空所に正しい語句を書き入れなさい。

1. A: Their website says they have only (　　　　　　　　　　).
   B: Then we can't (　　　　　　　　)! Make the reservation!

2. A: Sorry, but smartphones (　　　　　　　　　　) during the exam.
   B: I know, but I (　　　　　　　　　　) to use it for checking the time.

3. A: He (　　　　　　　　　) a job interview with Z Corporation.
   B: What a (　　　　　　　)!

## ❏ *Training B-2*:

90

英文を聴き、その英文に関する質問文の答えとして最も適切なものを (A)〜(D) より選びなさい。

**Question: Why did the speaker purchase the ticket?**

(A) A friend told him there were only a few available.

(B) It was inexpensive.

(C) Everyone said the concert was sold out.

(D) The chance was just too good.

91

## *Practice for Sound Change:* ［音変化に慣れよう］ フラッピング ①

「母音に挟まれ & 直前にアクセントがある t/d 音」の変化を扱います。

1. The maps show which areas will be below <u>water</u> by 2050.
2. You should not feel sorry that you did not <u>get a</u> gold <u>medal</u>.
3. They were getting a <u>lot of</u> applause and everyone seemed excited.
4. We were planning to visit more historical sites, but decided to <u>put it off</u> until tomorrow.
5. They say the terminal project will <u>exceed its</u> budget by millions of dollars.

# Exercises

**1.** 次の (1)〜(5) の英文を聴き取り、それぞれの空所に語句を書き入れなさい。

(1) Here are ten practical tips for (　　　　　　　　　　　　) at the theater.

(2) I will tell you how to take a video and (　　　　　　) YouTube.

(3) If you work hard, you can (　　　　　　　　　　) of success.

(4) I sometimes (　　　　　　　　) because I forget to charge my phone.

(5) She posted an open (　　　　　　　　　　) about her new album.


**2.** 次の (1), (2) の写真について、それぞれの写真を説明する英文が 4 つ聞こえてきます。
最も適切な英文の記号を○で囲みなさい。

(1)

(A)　(B)　(C)　(D)

(2)

(A)　(B)　(C)　(D)

64

**3.** 1.～3. の英文につづいて、(A), (B), (C) の 3 つの応答文が聞こえます。それぞれの英文の
応答文として最も適切な応答文の記号を○で囲みなさい。 🎵63

**1.** (A)　(B)　(C)
**2.** (A)　(B)　(C)
**3.** (A)　(B)　(C)

（Exercise 4 と Exercise 5 は解答提出問題です）

**4.** 会話文を聴き、その会話に関する質問文 (1), (2) の答えとして最も適切なものを (A)～(D)
より選び、巻末解答用紙の記号を○で囲みなさい。 🎵64

**(1)** According to this couple, what is the reaction to the performance?
- (A) Everyone but the critics loved it.
- (B) The audience liked it, but the couple did not.
- (C) Nobody enjoyed it, except the critics.
- (D) Everyone was crazy about it.

**(2)** What did the audience feel about the performance?
- (A) They loved it.
- (B) They hated it.
- (C) They agreed with the critics.
- (D) They were not allowed to watch.

**5.** 英文を聴き、その英文に関する質問文 (3), (4) の答えとして最も適切なものを (A)～(D) よ
り選び、巻末解答用紙の記号を○で囲みなさい。 🎵65

**(3)** How can one see the inner palace?
- (A) By wasting the opportunity
- (B) By viewing with other tourists
- (C) By arranging to see it in advance
- (D) By taking time to view it well

**(4)** Why should visitors take their time viewing the inner palace?
- (A) Only a small percentage can see it.
- (B) Taking pictures is not allowed.
- (C) No one is permitted to see it.
- (D) All the art work is original.

# Unit 14

# The tour comes with complimentary beverages.

**Points**

このユニットでは、「旅行・ホテル」に関する語句・表現と、「変化・移動・統一など」に関する語句・表現を聴き取る練習を行います。

## Section A  Travel/Hotel ［旅行・ホテル］

### ❏ *Key Words and Expressions*

92

1. **Attractions**（アトラクション）

   It's a nice hotel, but the area doesn't have many <u>attractions</u>.

2. **Book**（～を予約する）

   I tried to <u>book</u> a room at that hotel but they were full.

3. **Brochure**（パンフレット）

   Their <u>brochure</u> says they are only ten minutes away from the amusement park.

4. **Complimentary**（無料の）

   The tour comes with <u>complimentary</u> beverages.

5. **Feature**（～を呼び物にする）

   The spa <u>features</u> over ten different pools.

6. **Vacation**（休暇）

   He hasn't had a <u>vacation</u> in three years.

66

## ❑ *Training A-1*:

93

音声を聴いて空所に正しい語句を書き入れなさい。

1. A: Where are you going (　　　　　　　　　　　　) this year?
   B: I just (　　　　　　　　　) at a resort in Hawaii.

2. A: (　　　　　　　　　　) looks really nice.
   B: Yes, and there are so many (　　　　　　　　　　　).

3. A: The (　　　　　　　　　　) a hot-tub bath.
   B: Plus, they (　　　　　　　　　　　　) basket of fruit each morning.

## ❑ *Training A-2*:

94

会話文を聴き、その会話に関する質問文の答えとして最も適切なものを (A)〜(D) より選びなさい。

Question: What convinces the second speaker to select this hotel?
   (A) The nice brochure
   (B) Free transportation to the attractions
   (C) Complimentary entrance to the theme parks
   (D) Being distant from the attractions

## Section B   Change/Move/Make/Unite

[変化・移動・統一など]

## ❑ *Key Words and Expressions*

95

1. **Complete**（を完成させる）
   The new wing will not be <u>completed</u> until the spring.

2. **Head for**（〜へ向かう）
   Once you arrive, <u>head</u> straight <u>for</u> baggage claim.

3. **Improve**（向上する、進歩する）
   Service here has really <u>improved</u> under the new management.

4. **Organize**（〜を企画する、〜を計画する）
   She is trying to <u>organize</u> a going-away party for the boss.

**5. Raise / Reduce**（〜を上げる／〜を下げる）

I am hoping they will <u>reduce</u> the price after tourist season.

**6. Upgrade**（〜をアップグレードさせる、〜を向上させる）

Once I'm at the airport, I will try to <u>upgrade</u> my seat.

## ❑ *Training B-1*:

96

音声を聴いて空所に正しい語句を書き入れなさい。

1. A: They (                    ) the new highway next month.
   B: That should really (              ) to the mall.

2. A: Can I (              ) on my seat?
   B: Yes, but it will (          ) ticket price.

3. A: That's the last time I (              ) class reunion.
   B: Right. Too many (              ) straight for the bar.

## ❑ *Training B-2*:

97

英文を聴き、その英文に関する質問文の答えとして最も適切なものを (A) 〜 (D) より選びなさい。

**Question: What suggestion does the speaker have for the new hotel pool?**
   (A) He has no suggestion at all.
   (B) He would like more areas for children.
   (C) He would like a longer bar.
   (D) He would like less glare from the sun.

98

┌─────────────────────────────────────────────────────┐

*Practice for Sound Change:* ［音変化に慣れよう］ **フラッピング ②**

今回も「母音に挟まれ＆直前にアクセントがある t/d 音」の変化を扱います。

1. Our restaurant website is live! <u>Check it out</u> and tell us what you think.
2. In some cases, some change is <u>better</u> than none <u>at all</u>.
3. If you're angry, a crowded elevator is not exactly the best place to <u>let it all</u> out.
4. <u>Could I</u> leave my luggage here until check-in time?
5. Your marriage proposal might be more romantic if you <u>did it</u> while on vacation.

└─────────────────────────────────────────────────────┘

# Exercises

**1.** 次の (1)〜(5) の英文を聴き取り、それぞれの空所に語句を書き入れなさい。

(1) My grandfather and grandmother are wondering (　　　　　　　　　　) to live in an urban community.

(2) My wife and I love an ocean view. We always (　　　　　　　　　　) setting out for vacation.

(3) Take a deep breath and then (　　　　　　　　　　).

(4) "Are you scared of heights?" "(　　　　　　　　　　). I love riding roller coasters."

(5) What would you change if you (　　　　　　　　)?

**2.** 次の (1), (2) の写真について、それぞれの写真を説明する英文が 4 つ聞こえてきます。最も適切な英文の記号を○で囲みなさい。

(1)

(A)　(B)　(C)　(D)

(2)

(A)　(B)　(C)　(D)

**3.** 1.～3. の英文につづいて、(A), (B), (C) の3つの応答文が聞こえます。それぞれの英文の応答文として最も適切な応答文の記号を○で囲みなさい。 🅣68

1. (A)  (B)  (C)
2. (A)  (B)  (C)
3. (A)  (B)  (C)

(Exercise 4 と Exercise 5 は解答提出問題です)

**4.** 会話文を聴き、その会話に関する質問文 (1), (2) の答えとして最も適切なものを (A)～(D) より選び、巻末解答用紙の記号を○で囲みなさい。 🅣69

(1) Why is the party likely to improve this year?
    (A) Sandy is no longer in charge.
    (B) Sandy has more money to spend.
    (C) Sandy loves Halloween.
    (D) Sandy is new as the organizer.

(2) What is the man's opinion about last year's party?
    (A) It didn't improve.
    (B) It was lots of fun.
    (C) It didn't go well.
    (D) It was better than expected.

**5.** 英文を聴き、その英文に関する質問文 (3), (4) の答えとして最も適切なものを (A)～(D) より選び、巻末解答用紙の記号を○で囲みなさい。 🅣70

(3) What was wrong with the view?
    (A) It was not complimentary.
    (B) It was difficult to see.
    (C) It ended up being charged to the bill.
    (D) It took twice as long to see.

(4) What did the brochure say about the attractions?
    (A) They were nearby.
    (B) They were complimentary.
    (C) They would be charged to the bill.
    (D) They would take twice as long to reach.

# Unit 15

# There is too much competition in the retail clothing business.

**Points**

このユニットでは、「ビジネス・オフィス」に関する語句・表現と、「金銭関係」に関する語句・表現を聴き取る練習を行います。

## Section A Business/Office [ビジネス・オフィス]

### ❏ Key Words and Expressions

99

1. **Apply for**（〜に申し込む）
   I have <u>applied for</u> jobs at twelve different companies.

2. **Bid / Bid on**（入札価格／〜に入札する）
   We submitted a <u>bid</u> on that project, but didn't get it.

3. **Competition**（競争）
   There is too much <u>competition</u> in the retail clothing business.

4. **Cost**（コスト、経費）
   If we don't cut <u>costs</u>, we might go out of business.

5. **Hire**（〜を雇う）
   We haven't <u>hired</u> anyone new for four years.

6. **Profitable**（利益になる、もうかる）
   Our new tablet PCs have been very <u>profitable</u>.

## ❏ *Training A-1*:

100

音声を聴いて空所に正しい語句を書き入れなさい。

1. A: I heard you (                    ) at Custom Auto Service.
   B: Yeah, but I didn't (          ).

2. A: What makes your business (                )?
   B: We (              ) lower than those of (            ).

3. A: (              ) the new city hall project too?
   B: Of course, but (          ) was too high. Congratulations.

## ❏ *Training A-2*:

101

英文を聴き、その英文に関する質問文の答えとして最も適切なものを (A)〜(D) より選びなさい。

Question: What is one way this restaurant tries to keep costs down?
   (A) They apply for business loans.
   (B) They sell profitable items.
   (C) They pay low salaries.
   (D) They make big displays of well-selling items.

## Section B  Money Matters [金銭関係]

## ❏ *Key Words and Expressions*

102

1. **Budget**（予算）
   We have no <u>budget</u> for building repairs this year.

2. **Cover the costs**（費用をまかなう）
   The bonus amount will <u>cover the costs</u> of our new patio.

3. **Deposit**（を預金する）
   My salary is <u>deposited</u> directly into my bank account.

4. **Estimate**（見積もり）
   I asked for an <u>estimate</u> on redesigning our website.

72

5. Fee（料金、〜料）

Their repair <u>fee</u> was far beyond what I could afford.

6. Rate（率、割合）

If interest <u>rates</u> drop, I might apply for a loan.

## ❑ *Training B-1:*

103

音声を聴いて空所に正しい語句を書き入れなさい。

1. A: Do we have enough left (　　　　　　　　　　) roof repair?
   B: Maybe. Ask for a (　　　　　　　　) and we can think about it.

2. A: The (　　　　　　　　) is going down.
   B: That makes our (　　　　　　　　) a little cheaper.

3. A: How much do (　　　　　　　　　　) in the bank?
   B: Not (　　　　　　　　　　) of a new computer system.

## ❑ *Training B-2:*

104

会話文を聴き、その会話に関する質問文の答えとして最も適切なものを (A)〜(D) より選びなさい。

Question: What is wrong with the current estimate?
    (A) It won't cover the cost.
    (B) It is under their budget.
    (C) It is more than they can afford.
    (D) It's not as good as other estimates.

105

## *Practice for Sound Change:* ［音変化に慣れよう］ フラッピング ③

今回も「母音 +[t/d] 音 +[l] 音」で起きる音変化を扱います。

1. Currently we have raised a <u>little</u> more than 15% of the total budget.
2. We support those fighting the physical and financial <u>battle</u> against cancer.
3. My car broke down in the <u>middle</u> of nowhere, with <u>little</u> chance of finding a hotel.
4. He returned to Minnesota to <u>handle</u> the family's business affairs.
5. When the dollar fell below 100 yen, it <u>startled</u> the market.

# Exercises

**1.** 次の (1)〜(5) の英文を聴き取り、それぞれの空所に語句を書き入れなさい。

(1) (                    ) complimentary water will be provided on the tour.

(2) Our website will tell you a few steps that can (                    ) at your new office.

(3) To research (                    ) their nesting grounds will require a large budget.

(4) Malaysian (                    ) receive gold bars worth an estimated $600,000.

(5) (                    ) will be upgraded but I won't get a pay raise.

**2.** 次の (1), (2) の写真について、それぞれの写真を説明する英文が 4 つ聞こえてきます。最も適切な英文の記号を○で囲みなさい。

(1)

(A)　(B)　(C)　(D)

(2)

(A)　(B)　(C)　(D)

**3.** 1.～3. の英文につづいて、(A), (B), (C) の 3 つの応答文が聞こえます。それぞれの英文の応答文として最も適切な応答文の記号を○で囲みなさい。

**1.** (A)　(B)　(C)
**2.** (A)　(B)　(C)
**3.** (A)　(B)　(C)

（Exercise 4 と Exercise 5 は解答提出問題です）

**4.** 会話文を聴き、その会話に関する質問文 (1), (2) の答えとして最も適切なものを (A)～(D) より選び、巻末解答用紙の記号を○で囲みなさい。

**(1)** What does the wife want her husband to do?
　　(A) Get a job with the competition
　　(B) Apply for another job
　　(C) Hire a member of her family
　　(D) Help her nephew join a competing company

**(2)** What was wrong with the job application?
　　(A) It was made by the woman's nephew.
　　(B) It wasn't on time.
　　(C) It was for a competitor.
　　(D) It was for the wrong job.

**5.** 英文を聴き、その英文に関する質問文 (3), (4) の答えとして最も適切なものを (A)～(D) より選び、巻末解答用紙の記号を○で囲みなさい。

**(3)** Why will the lower exchange rate help this company?
　　(A) Analysts say this trend will continue.
　　(B) Some branches need software upgrades.
　　(C) The company has significant deposits overseas.
　　(D) The company will now pay more taxes.

**(4)** What will happen next year?
　　(A) The exchange rate will remain favorable.
　　(B) The exchange rate will result in a different situation.
　　(C) The exchange rate will decrease the value of overseas savings.
　　(D) The exchange rate will allow for software upgrades.

Keys to Listening Success
場面・機能・音変化で学ぶ実践リスニング

編著者　　　西 谷 恒 志

　　　　　　トム・ディロン

発行者　　　山 口 隆 史

発 行 所　　　　株式会社 音羽書房鶴見書店

〒113-0033　東京都文京区本郷 3-26-13
TEL 03-3814-0491
FAX 03-3814-9250
URL: http://www.otowatsurumi.com
e-mail: info@otowatsurumi.com

2022 年 3 月 1 日　　初版発行
2022 年 10 月 1 日　　2 刷発行

組版・装幀　ほんのしろ
印刷・製本　(株)シナノ
■ 落丁・乱丁本はお取り替えいたします。

EC-076

## UNIT 6  Answer Sheet

4. (1) (A) (B) (C) (D)    Score:
   (2) (A) (B) (C) (D)

5. (3) (A) (B) (C) (D)
   (4) (A) (B) (C) (D)

ID:

Name:                         Month/Date/Year:


## UNIT 1  Answer Sheet

4. (1) (A) (B) (C) (D)    Score:
   (2) (A) (B) (C) (D)

5. (3) (A) (B) (C) (D)
   (4) (A) (B) (C) (D)

ID:

Name:                         Month/Date/Year:


## UNIT 7  Answer Sheet

4. (1) (A) (B) (C) (D)    Score:
   (2) (A) (B) (C) (D)

5. (3) (A) (B) (C) (D)
   (4) (A) (B) (C) (D)

ID:

Name:                         Month/Date/Year:


## UNIT 2  Answer Sheet

4. (1) (A) (B) (C) (D)    Score:
   (2) (A) (B) (C) (D)

5. (3) (A) (B) (C) (D)
   (4) (A) (B) (C) (D)

ID:

Name:                         Month/Date/Year:


## UNIT 8  Answer Sheet

4. (1) (A) (B) (C) (D)    Score:
   (2) (A) (B) (C) (D)

5. (3) (A) (B) (C) (D)
   (4) (A) (B) (C) (D)

ID:

Name:                         Month/Date/Year:


## UNIT 3  Answer Sheet

4. (1) (A) (B) (C) (D)    Score:
   (2) (A) (B) (C) (D)

5. (3) (A) (B) (C) (D)
   (4) (A) (B) (C) (D)

ID:

Name:                         Month/Date/Year:


## UNIT 9  Answer Sheet

4. (1) (A) (B) (C) (D)    Score:
   (2) (A) (B) (C) (D)

5. (3) (A) (B) (C) (D)
   (4) (A) (B) (C) (D)

ID:

Name:                         Month/Date/Year:


## UNIT 4  Answer Sheet

4. (1) (A) (B) (C) (D)    Score:
   (2) (A) (B) (C) (D)

5. (3) (A) (B) (C) (D)
   (4) (A) (B) (C) (D)

ID:

Name:                         Month/Date/Year:


## UNIT 10  Answer Sheet

4. (1) (A) (B) (C) (D)    Score:
   (2) (A) (B) (C) (D)

5. (3) (A) (B) (C) (D)
   (4) (A) (B) (C) (D)

ID:

Name:                         Month/Date/Year:


## UNIT 5  Answer Sheet

4. (1) (A) (B) (C) (D)    Score:
   (2) (A) (B) (C) (D)

5. (3) (A) (B) (C) (D)
   (4) (A) (B) (C) (D)

ID:

Name:                         Month/Date/Year:

## UNIT 11 Answer Sheet

**4.** (1)  (A)  (B)  (C)  (D)

    (2)  (A)  (B)  (C)  (D)

**5.** (3)  (A)  (B)  (C)  (D)

    (4)  (A)  (B)  (C)  (D)

Score:

ID:

Name:

Month/Date/Year:

## UNIT 12 Answer Sheet

**4.** (1)  (A)  (B)  (C)  (D)

    (2)  (A)  (B)  (C)  (D)

**5.** (3)  (A)  (B)  (C)  (D)

    (4)  (A)  (B)  (C)  (D)

Score:

ID:

Name:

Month/Date/Year:

## UNIT 13 Answer Sheet

**4.** (1)  (A)  (B)  (C)  (D)

    (2)  (A)  (B)  (C)  (D)

**5.** (3)  (A)  (B)  (C)  (D)

    (4)  (A)  (B)  (C)  (D)

Score:

ID:

Name:

Month/Date/Year:

## UNIT 14 Answer Sheet

**4.** (1)  (A)  (B)  (C)  (D)

    (2)  (A)  (B)  (C)  (D)

**5.** (3)  (A)  (B)  (C)  (D)

    (4)  (A)  (B)  (C)  (D)

Score:

ID:

Name:

Month/Date/Year:

## UNIT 15 Answer Sheet

**4.** (1)  (A)  (B)  (C)  (D)

    (2)  (A)  (B)  (C)  (D)

**5.** (3)  (A)  (B)  (C)  (D)

    (4)  (A)  (B)  (C)  (D)

Score:

ID:

Name:

Month/Date/Year: